"I'm big enough to admit that I am often inspired by myself."

— Leslie Knope

Parks and Interrogation

A Parks & Recreation Quiz Book

Published by Beartown Press

Contents

Introduction

Parks and Recreation is one of the most-loved sitcoms of modern times. 'Loved' is a suitable adjective for the show; it's hilarious without malice, the characters care about each other and are (mostly) incredibly passionate about what they do.

From Leslie and Ron to Andy and Chris, it's a show full of people you'd like to be friends with. It's more than just a sitcom; it's frequently incredibly touching, meaningful and optimistic. And funny. Very, very funny. That's why we love it, and it's why this quiz book exists.

Here's what you have on your hands:

- 405 quiz questions about Parks and Recreation

- The questions are separated into 26 themed rounds, plus an extra set of tiebreakers to separate the Knopes from the nopes

- Each round is made up of 15 questions

- Answer sheets for each round are located in the second half of the book

- If you haven't seen all of Parks and Rec, please be aware that this book contains spoilers (obviously)

So, if you're ready to prove who should ascend to the peak of the Ron Swanson Pyramid of Greatness, and who should be recalled from city council let's get started...

Season 1

1. In the pilot episode, what injury has Andy sustained by falling into the pit?

2. What is the name of the town planner on whom Leslie has a crush?

3. Shauna Mulwae-Tweep arrives at city council to interview members of the team about the pit construction project. What newspaper does she work for?

4. How many friends has the pit construction project earned on social media when the team first check it?

5. What gift to the department does Leslie initially confiscate as it is over $25 in value, but later enjoy, partially resulting in a letter being put on her file?

6. What possession of Andy's does Ann's neighbour steal from her house, prompting an injured, nude Andy to chase him through the street?

7. Tom tried to curry favour with Ron by deliberately losing to him at a particular online game. What is that game?

8. What are the group of teenage boys throwing at each other when Leslie and Tom arrive to intervene?

9. What does Ron describe as "my number one favourite food, wrapped around my number three favourite food" while attending the awards banquet?

10. Who does Ron present an award to at the banquet?

11. What pick-up artist technique does Tom claim to be using, when he wears a goofy orange hat at the bar?

12. Tom's wife Wendy is introduced in the season finale. What is her job?

13. What does an annoyed Ann learn from a doctor at the hospital, in relation to Andy's recovery?

14. How old is George Gernway, the man Leslie's mother sets her up on a date with?

15. Who falls into the pit at the end of the season?

Answers on page 86

Leslie

How well do you know the hardest-working woman in Pawnee-based politics?

1. What is Leslie's job title in the early seasons of the show?

2. Where does Ben propose to Leslie?

3. What is the subtitle to Leslie's book about Pawnee?

4. Name three of the five women whose photographs Leslie displays on the wall next to her door.

5. How many shots of espresso does Leslie have in her coffee?

6. In which fictional town was Leslie Knope born?

7. What is Leslie Knope's mother's name?

8. Who does the online dating service match Leslie with?

9. By what slender margin does Leslie beat Bobby Newport in the Season 4 city council election?

10. What type of animal does Leslie find "condescending"?

11. What is Leslie's favourite restaurant?

12. When Andy is assigning code names to the group during the bus tour, what name does he give Leslie?

13. Which former First Lady has Leslie met?

14. Who is number one on Leslie's 'sex list'?

15. What are the names of Leslie and Ben's three children?

Answers on page 89

Tom's Business Ideas

Tom's business ideas were as plentiful as they were flawed. But can you remember what each business did from the name alone?

1. Snake Juice.

2. Saltweens.

3. Club-A-Dub-Dub or Clubmarine.

4. Entertainment 720.

5. Snail Mail.

6. Sparkle Suds.

7. Disco Dairy.

8. Tommy Fresh.

9. Eclipse.

10. H2HO.

11. Rent-a-Swag.

12. Yogurt Platinum.

13. Tommy and the Foxx.

14. Talking Tissues.

15. Know Ya Boo.

Answers on page 92

Ron

A titan among men, a lover of steak and perhaps the toughest man ever to have been given the name Ronald. How well do you know Ron Swanson?

1. What is the name of Ron's jazz saxophonist alter ego?

2. Who is Tammy Zero, in relation to Ron?

3. What is Ron's middle name?

4. How old was Ron when he began work in a sheet metal factory?

5. Tom reveals that when Ron has sex, he dresses like which sportsman the next day?

6. What snack is known as a "Swanson" around Pawnee?

7. How does Ron summarise his hamburger 'recipe'?

8. What is Ron's wife called?

9. Which family member does Ron reference when asked if his family had any history of mental illness?

10. Ron claims to have cried only twice. When?

11. How many toes does Ron have?

12. What was the name of the building company run by Ron in Season 7?

13. What does Ron say is the only thing he hates more than lying?

14. What is Ron's ringtone?

15. Which tennis star does Ron list as being one of his ideal women?

<u>Answers on page 95</u>

Season 2

1. How does Leslie cause controversy at Pawnee Zoo?

2. What do Leslie and Tom discover has been planted in the new community garden?

3. Which two justifications does Councilman Bill Dexhart offer after he is found to have been engaging in four-way sex in a Brazilian cave while he was supposed to be building houses for the underprivileged?

4. The Parks and Recreation department receives international visitors from a twin city of Pawnee. What country are the visitors from?

5. What is the name of the charity which arrives in Pawnee to build a playground in a single day?

6. Why does Ron keep visiting Andy for shoe-shines?

7. Which two members of the department are on the judging panel of the annual Miss Pawnee beauty pageant?

8. What dinosaur-themed restaurant do the gang go to for a night out after Tom's divorce?

9. Which member of the department discovers Ron's secret (jazz-related) double life, following a tip-off?

10. Which two characters appear in the cover photo of the Summer Events Catalog?

11. Which of the following do not visit Leslie's house during the party in which she is trying to impress Justin? A judo master.

12. Who wins the Woman of the Year award?

13. On which date does April schedule 94 meetings for Ron, believing (incorrectly) that the date doesn't exist?

14. The penultimate episode of Season 2 sees two new characters join the show. Who are they?

15. What is the name of the performer hired to sing at the annual children's concert?

Answers on page 98

April

She's the master of deadpan and the personification of the word 'apathetic', but how much do you know about April Ludgate?

1. How old is April in Season 1?

2. What did April want to be as a child?

3. What is April's sister called?

4. What does April do for Andy to help make Ann jealous?

5. What is April's middle name, as revealed at her wedding to Andy?

6. What was Andy's somewhat underwhelming reply when April said "I love you"?

7. April created her own major in college. What was it?

8. How long does April date Andy before they get married?

9. What language does April speak (apart from English)?

10. Where does April move to during Season 5?

11. What is the name of the three-legged dog adopted by April and Andy?

12. What was the name of April's bisexual boyfriend?

13. What nickname did April's parents give her: TuTu, WuWu or ZuZu?

14. What Halloween-friendly song was playing when April gave birth?

15. What is the name of April and Andy's son?

Answers on page 101

Who Said It?

Can you remember who delivered these classic Parks and Recreation lines?

1. "Just remember, every time you look up at the moon, I, too, will be looking at a moon. Not the same moon, obviously, That's impossible."

2. "These dogs are so cute I want to throw up and kill myself."

3. "Oh my god! [catches calculator] Hey, Dr. Buttons! …I mean, my old calculator. It doesn't have a name."

4. "No matter what I do, literally nothing bad can happen to me. I'm like a white, male US Senator."

5. "If I keep my body moving, and my mind occupied at all times, I will avoid falling into a bottomless pit of despair."

6. "When Andy and I used to go the movies, he would always try to guess the ending of the movie. And he would always guess that the main character had been dead the whole time. Even when we saw Ratatouille."

7. "I once worked with a guy for three years and never learned his name. Best friend I ever had. We still never talk sometimes."

8. "Do I look like I drink water?"

9. "Most people would say 'the deets', but I say 'the tails'. Just another example of innovation."

10. "I didn't know I was adopted."

11. "Let the record show there was a standing ovation."

12. "Boss man, I wanna go home early. Ooh, hold on actually, hang on. Yeah, no, I wanna quit and never come here again."

13. "I guess my thoughts on abortion are, you know, let's all just have a good time."

14. "Thank god my grandfather just died, so I am fluh-uh-shed with ca-ah-ash."

15. "I wasn't listening but I strongly disagree with Ann."

Answers on page 104

Andy

A round dedicated to the man with the mind of a puppy, the body of Star-Lord and the singing voice of a nightingale full of gravel. How much do you know about Andy Dwyer?

1. What is the main name of Andy's band?

2. What is the name of Andy's FBI alter ego?

3. Who was Andy's most regular customer at the shoeshine stand (though rarely received great customer service)?

4. Which landmark do Andy and April visit in Season 3?

5. What is the age gap between Andy and April?

6. What does Andy diagnose Leslie with after trying to look up her symptoms on the internet?

7. What did Andy claim was his favourite food?

8. Andy didn't actually sell his last car - what happened to it?

9. Which part of the police entry examination does Andy fail: the physical test, the personality test or the written test?

10. What is Andy's favourite football team?

11. What song did Andy write to celebrate the life of Li'l Sebastian?

12. What did Andy study at college?

13. What is the full name of Andy's children's entertainment television show?

14. Which British aristocrat does Andy befriend in Season 6?

15. How does Andy explain his significant weight loss in Season 6?

Answers on page 107

Season 3

1. Which two characters go head-to-head as coaches of Pawnee's only two junior league basketball teams?

2. What is the only item placed in the time capsule?

3. Which member of the Parks department does Ann bump into at the singles' mixer?

4. Where does Tom pitch his cologne to Dennis Feinstein?

5. Leslie discovers a woman's razor and a pink swimming cap in Chris's bathroom, resulting in her telling Ann he is having an affair. What is Chris's explanation for the presence of the items?

6. Which radio duo catch Ben off-guard during an interview with questions about his time as a teenage mayor?

7. Which Pawnee event does Leslie resurrect to help get the Parks department budget restored?

8. Where does Ron reveal that he tends to buy most of his food?

9. Ron begins Season 3 dating Tom ex-wife Wendy, but they break up when she moves away. What country does she relocate to?

10. Who paints a depiction of Leslie as a powerful and bare-chested Greek goddess?

11. What fitting birthday party does Leslie throw for Ron?

12. Which band does April (briefly) tell Andy is her favourite (rather than his band)?

13. What does young girl Lauren write in response to her assignment "Why Government Matters", after spending the afternoon with Ron?

14. What does Ron offer as a gift to Lauren to help her protect her property?

15. Who gets singed by a fireball while attempting to light the eternal flame at Li'l Sebastian's memorial?

Answers on page 110

Tom

Pawnee's most tenacious businessman is known (primarily to himself) as "the brown Gosling", but what else do you know about him?

1. Which state is Tom from?

2. Which sport's reservation system does Tom have complete authority over, allowing him to meet female guests?

3. Tom states that one of his pickup tactics is to give girls copies of his house keys and tell them to show up whenever. He says that no one has shown up so far, but how many times has he been robbed?

4. Where does Tom meet Lucy, who he is dating as of the Season 7 finale?

5. Which of his colleagues does Tom accidentally shoot during the hunting trip?

6. What is the primary reason for Tom and Wendy getting divorced?

7. Which retail store is Tom working at, at the beginning of Season 3?

8. Who does Tom sell the Rent-a-Swag business to?

9. Why does Leslie match with Tom on the online dating service?

10. What is the name of the restaurant Tom opens?

11. What name does Tom give his vacuum-cleaning, music-playing creation?

12. Where does Tom eventually take inspiration from when designing the new Parks department logo?

13. What does Tom claim is behind every successful man?

14. How does Tom propose to Lucy?

15. What was his original plan for the proposal?

Answers on page 113

The Ron Swanson Pyramid of Greatness

Can you tell which of the following traits feature in the Ron Swanson Pyramid of Greatness, and which ones are made-up?

1. Canada.

2. Crying.

3. Torso.

4. Sickness Management.

5. Shelving.

6. Biceps.

7. Firearms.

8. Deer Protein.

9. Stillness.

10. Romantic Love.

11. Testicles.

12. Ability to Create Fire.

13. Gold.

14. Old Wooden Sailing Ships.

15. Poise.

Answers on page 116

Chris

Scientists believe that the first human being who will live 150 years has already been born. Chris believes that human being is him. But what else do you literally know about Mr Traeger?

1. What is the name of Chris's therapist?

2. What does Chris say is his resting heart rate: 13, 23 or 33 beats per minute?

3. What event from his past does Chris put his relentless positivity down to?

4. Who does Chris go to Andy and April's Halloween party dressed as?

5. What is the name of Jerry's daughter, whom Chris dates for a while?

6. What is Chris's job when he first enters the show?

7. And what job does he take, that sees him stay in Pawnee more permanently?

8. What is Chris's body fat percentage? (We'll accept the nearest whole number if you want to guess.)

9. What type of burger does Chris make in an (unsuccessful) attempt to beat Ron's hamburger?

10. What is unusual about the new desk Chris gives to Ron?

11. When Andy assigns each member of the department a code name during the bus tour, what does he label Chris?

12. When Ann confronts Chris about her suspicions that he is cheating on her, he is surprised. Why?

13. What 'candy' does Chris offer the group when they are waiting hungrily for Ron's barbecue?

14. When Chris is preparing to move back to Indianapolis, who does he ask to come with him?

15. What song does Chris use to showcase his (limited) vocal abilities when acting as a backing vocalist on Andy's campaign song?

Answers on page 118

Season 4

1. What is the name of the youth camp run by Leslie?

2. Who emails a photograph of their genitals to all of the female employees at City Hall?

3. How long does Ron go to hide in the wilderness for, after learning Tammy One has arrived in town?

4. How does Leslie escape more severe punishment for her secret relationship with Ben?

5. Which territory does April play as in the Model United Nations conference?

6. What gift is Ben trying to give Leslie when she flees into the woods to hide with Ron?

7. What is the name of Leslie's campaign song, written by Andy?

8. How long is the claymation film produced by Ben when he premieres it to Chris?

9. What is the name of Bobby Newport's campaign manager?

10. What alcohol do Tammy Zero and Tammy One use for their "prairie drink-off"?

11. April drives Andy to see the Grand Canyon to check off one of his bucket-list items, but what landmark was he actually thinking of?

12. Who does Ann go on a date with on Valentine's Day?

13. Who was the pie that hits Jerry in the face actually intended for?

14. Whose birthday gets forgotten (and belatedly celebrated) during Leslie's campaign?

15. Who accidentally deletes all of the department's files?

Answers on page 121

Ben

Known as everything from The Architect to the man who tamed the wild, wild heart of Leslie Knope, how well do you know Mr. Ben Wyatt?

1. What town was Ben elected mayor of while still a teenager?

2. How did he accidentally bankrupt the city?

3. What is Ben's favourite food?

4. What nickname does Jean-Ralphio give Ben?

5. When Andy assigns each member of the department a code name during the bus tour, what is Ben given?

6. What does Ben buy to cheer himself up while on a "Treat Yo' Self" outing with Donna and Tom?

7. What is the name of the claymation film Ben works on during downtime after his resignation?

8. What fantasy memorabilia item does Leslie gift to Ben for their anniversary?

9. Who does Ben take on as his assistant when he starts working for Sweetums?

10. With which Cones of Dunshire piece does Ben ultimately beat Gryzzl's founder in their duel to get Pawnee accepted into Gryzzl's WiFi initiative?

11. Which board game is Ben a "nationally ranked" player of?

12. What authoritarian figures does Ben have a huge fear of?

13. Who does Ben spend his and Leslie's first anniversary with, enjoying a couple's massage, a horse-drawn carriage ride and tango lessons?

14. What does the accounting firm give Ben as a leaving present?

15. What British honour is bestowed on Ben by Lord Covington in The Johnny Karate Super Awesome Musical Explosion Show?

Answers on page 124

Andy's Band Names

Can you tell the real names of Andy's bands from the ones we've made up?

1. Crackfinger.

2. Frightshaft.

3. Threeskin.

4. Ninjadick.

5. Ham Dragon.

6. Psych Ass.

7. Jet Black Pope.

8. God Hates Figs.

9. Department of Homeland Obscurity.

10. The Kind Man's Cruellest Secret.

11. Muscle Confusion.

12. The Museum of Natural Fistery.

13. Flames for Flames.

14. Man Feelings.

15. The Clone Harbourers.

Answers on page 127

Donna

"I have several men in rotation. One's waiting for me out in the car. Don't worry, I rolled down the window." Just how well do you know Pawnee's own "Treat Yo' Self" queen, Donna Meagle?

1. What is Donna's job in the Parks department?

2. What is the name of Donna's famous musician cousin?

3. What type of car does Donna own?

4. Which band wrote an album about Donna, as revealed at her wedding to Joe?

5. What type of business does Donna found on leaving the Parks department? (Bonus point if you can remember the name of the business.)

6. What does Donna work as between the government shutdown and its reopening in the opening episode of Season 3?

7. Donna's grandma was a fan of the menfolk, and her dating advice to Donna was "use him, abuse him, lose him". But how did she die?

8. What is Donna's husband's job?

9. What is Donna's simple rule when it comes to dating football players?

10. Legally, what is the maximum number of members of Donna's family that can be on an international flight together at the same time?

11. What is Donna's favourite TV show, which she bonds with Craig over?

12. Which feature of which character, combined with Donna's "everything else", would make their hypothetical child unstoppable?

13. What is the name of Donna's (and Ron's) hairdresser, who later marries Craig Middlebrooks?

14. What is the name of Donna's brother, whom she hates?

15. Which Oscar-winning actress auditioned for the role of Donna?

Answers on page 129

Season 5

1. Whose words of comfort does Leslie rebuff while sulking in the coatroom at a cocktail party?

2. What is the name of the pig which Ron brings to the barbecue?

3. How does Ron meet Diane?

4. What does April want to turn Lot 48 into?

5. What is the first (sugar-related) bill Leslie tries to pass in city council?

6. How do Leslie and April manage to dispose of the huge refrigerator the garbage team were unable to lift?

7. What does April give Leslie as a present after their time spent working as garbage collectors?

8. Ron, Chris and Ben all catch food-poisoning when choosing a caterer for the wedding. Why is Tom, who was also in attendance, unaffected?

9. Which potential candidate announces Ann's sperm donor hunt on the radio?

10. Where do Leslie and Ben get married?

11. Who crashes the wedding, before being gently suppressed by Ron?

12. What is the name of the business that pops up to rival Rent-a-Swag?

13. What does Chris tell Ann is his spirit animal: a jaguar, a lion, a woodmouse or a hare?

14. Who does Ann ultimately decide to have a baby with?

15. What type of business does Leslie bail out, resulting in it taking a somewhat seedier direction?

Answers on page 132

Garry

He is perhaps both the kindest-hearted and unluckiest man in Pawnee. How well do you know Garry/Jerry/Terry/Larry/Barry?

1. What is Garry's actual first name? (Clue: it isn't Garry.)

2. What is Garry's wife named?

3. How many daughters does Garry have?

4. In Season 2, an injured Garry claims to have been mugged in the park. What really happened?

5. What year was Garry born: 1948, 1950 or 1952?

6. Ron describes Garry (then Jerry) as both the "schlemiel" and the "schlemazel" of the office. What does this mean?

7. What misdemeanour does policeman Dave reveal Jerry has committed on a number of occasions?

8. What is Garry's favourite holiday destination?

9. When Garry suffered a heart attack and extreme flatulence simultaneously after being surprised by Leslie and Ann, what was Tom's diagnosis?

10. Why did Donna, Tom, Andy and April not receive their invitations to Garry's family party?

11. What musical instrument does Garry play?

12. What does Garry accidentally get printed as the background image on Tom's restaurant menus?

13. What date is Garry's birthday?

14. How many terms does Garry go on to serve as mayor of Pawnee?

15. True or false: Garry's surname is spelt incorrectly on his headstone?

Answers on page 135

Anagrams

Can you solve these anagrams to reveal the names of the Parks and Recreation characters?

1. Overdraft Ohm?

2. Be Brown By Pot?

3. Managed Lone?

4. Graduate Pill?

5. Spanner Ink?

6. New Batty?

7. Yawned Dry?

8. China Mop?

9. Elope Likens?

10. Right Careers?

11. Liable Stains?

12. Hardly Peep?

13. Sworn Anons?

14. Canola Jazz Mole?

15. Gig Rag Cherry?

Answers on page 138

Tom's Nicknames for Things

Because Tom is cool, he doesn't always call things by their standard names. Can you tell what he would be referring to if he was to use the below terminology?

1. "Zerts".

2. "Tray-trays".

3. "Sammies".

4. "Big ol' cookies".

5. "Cool blasterz".

6. "Sandoozles".

7. "Long ass rice".

8. "Fri-fri chicky-chick".

9. "Chicky catch".

10. "Adam Sandlers".

11. "Pre-birds".

12. "Super water".

13. "Bean blankies".

14. "Food rakes".

15. "Go-go mobile".

Answers on page 140

Season 6

1. What city do Leslie, Ben, Ron, April and Andy visit for the first two episodes?

2. Who is maid of honour at Ron and Diane's wedding?

3. Where do Ann and Chris move to from Pawnee?

4. Who accidentally uses the Parks department's Twitter handle for a sex-themed tweet?

5. Why does Tom decide to get his wine cellar soundproofed?

6. What is released when Leslie tears down the wall separating Pawnee and Eagleton?

7. What does Ann name her baby?

8. What is the name of Annabel Porter's internet lifestyle magazine that labels Ron's handmade chairs as a trend?

9. What does April finally decide is Donna's spirit dog?

10. What do Ron and Diane name their son?

11. Who comes up with Andy's stage name when he's providing children's entertainment?

12. What do the guys gift to Chris as a leaving present?

13. Which local celebrity do Leslie and Ann get to endorse the new Sweetums sports drink, as part of the chain of events that will allow them to gain access to Lot 48?

14. Which musical event takes place at the finale of the season?

15. And which establishment holds its grand opening shortly after that event?

Answers on page 142

Leslie's Romantic Descriptions of Ann

Leslie and Ann are perhaps TV's greatest female friendship. But can you tell Leslie's real descriptions of Ann from the ones we've made up?

1. "Ann, you beautiful tropical fish."

2. "Ann, you beautiful, naive, sophisticated newborn baby."

3. "Ann, you wistful, fragrant tiger lily."

4. "Ann, you cunning, pliable, chestnut-haired sunfish."

5. "Ann, you rainbow-infused space unicorn."

6. "Ann, you freshly-bathed crab-hustler."

7. "Ann, you beautiful spinster."

8. "Ann, you opalescent tree-shark."

9. "Ann, you benevolent, whispering clam."

10. "Ann, you poetic, noble land-mermaid."

11. "Ann, you heroic, gloriously-tousled capybara."

12. "Ann, you rare, glorious deer-queen."

13. "Ann, you glossy, Parisian sea-otter."

14. "Ann, you beautiful, rule-breaking moth."

15. "Ann, you beautiful, talented, brilliant, powerful musk-ox."

Answers on page 145

Complete the Quote

Can you fill in the gaps in these classic Parks & Recreation quotes?

1. "Strippers do nothing for me…but I will take a _____ _____ _____ anytime, anyplace." - Ron.

2. "We have to remember what's important in life: friends, _____ and work. Or _____, friends and work. But work has to come third." - Leslie.

3. "Sometimes you gotta work a little so you can _____ a lot." - Tom.

4. "I think that _____ _____ always screams 'fun', right?" - Jerry/Garry.

5. "I don't know who _____ _____ is, and at this point I'm too afraid to ask." - Andy.

6. "It's like I always say. When life gives you lemons, you sell some of your _____'s _____, and go clubbing." - Jean-Ralphio.

7. "Crying: Acceptable at funerals and the _____ _____." - Ron.

8. "I made my money the old-fashioned way. I got run over by a _____!" - Jean-Ralphio.

9. "On a scale from one to _____ _____, how p*ssed off is he?" - Tom.

10. "No offence, but I don't remember you having a nursing degree in _____." - Leslie.

11. "It's like dealing with a strict mother. Who I am confusingly attracted to. Ben is like _____ _____." - Leslie.

12. "I don't get anything until I'm 50, which is a waste because I'm going to be a billionaire in Costa Rica by then. Eatin' dolphin and hangin' out with _____ _____." - Jean-Ralphio.

13. "April is the best. But she's 20. When April was born, I was already in the third grade, which means if we were friends back then, I would have been hanging out with a baby. I don't know anything about _____ _____." - Andy.

14. "As Leslie's Maid of Honor, I really need her bachelorette party to go well, which is why I'm stress-eating these _____ _____." - Ann.

15. "I love Chinese crap. Lucy Liu, Gangnam Style, Nintendo, _____, etc, etc." - Jeremy Jamm.

Answers on page 147

Season 7

1. What was the Morning Star referenced in the "Morning Star Incident"?

2. What is the value of the bid Leslie places to buy land from the wealthy Newport family to create a national park?

3. Who is seduced by Tammy Two?

4. Who gets inducted into the Pawnee "Walk of Fame"?

5. What is the name of the tech company that begins to take over Pawnee?

6. What is the name of Tammy Two's perfume?

7. Who is Donna's maid of honour?

8. Which two characters pass away in the episode 'Two Funerals'?

9. Who becomes the new landlord of JJ's Diner?

10. Who manages to negotiate ownership of the rights to Johnny Karate for Andy?

11. Which of these items did not appear on Craig's list of Great Things About Being Alive: watermelon martinis, exposed brick, Jennifer Love Hewitt or air-dried beech beams?

12. In the finale, who is shown to go on to become a best-selling author?

13. Which two characters fake their own deaths, before turning up at their own funeral?

14. What is the name of the online learning initiative Donna sets up with her husband?

15. What is the final line spoken in the season, by Leslie?

Answers on page 150

Cast & Crew

A round all about the talented people behind Parks and Recreation.

1. Which two people created the show?

2. Who was the first main cast member to direct an episode?

3. Which Mad Men star cameos as an incompetent member of the National Parks Service?

4. Who plays Chris Traeger?

5. Who plays Ann Perkins?

6. Who plays Tom Haverford?

7. Who plays Bobby Newport?

8. Which two Brooklyn Nine-Nine stars cameo?

9. Who plays Ben Wyatt?

10. Which Good Place star appears in Parks and Recreation as an Eagleton councilwoman?

11. What was considered as a title for the sitcom, before being rejected by network executives who didn't want to make fun of local government?

12. Which Arrested Development star appears as an MRI consultant who goes on a date with Leslie?

13. Who cameos during one of Tom and Donna's Treat Yo' Self days, ordering the sushi named after himself at a Beverly Hills restaurant?

14. Who plays Donna Meagle?

15. Which network did Seasons 1-7 originally air on?

Answers on page 153

Special

In April 2020, the cast of Parks and Recreation reprised their roles for a special fundraising episode created during the coronavirus pandemic.

1. What date in 2020 did the episode air?

2. Who is the first character to appear in the special?

3. What platform are the group using to carry out their video calls?

4. Who keeps getting skipped over in the call tree?

5. What service does Jeremy Jamm advertise?

6. While under the influence of cleaning supplies, Ben plans to combine two of his greatest creations during lockdown. What does he plan to make?

7. How frequently is Chris donating blood?

8. And what does Chris say is his blood type?

9. Where is Andy trapped?

10. Who keeps accidentally applying filters to their video calls?

11. Where in the world does Tom claim to be, with the assistance of a virtual background?

12. What illustrious collective of awards does Joan Calamezzo claim to have obtained?

13. During the video calls, what is on the shelves behind Donna (when she doesn't join Tom in the virtual background destination)?

14. Which intruder did Ron catch in his cabin?

15. Which song do the characters sing for Leslie at the end of the episode?

<u>Answers on page 156</u>

Tiebreakers

Tied at the end of your quiz? Here's some "closest to" questions to help separate the wheat from the chaff.

1. Including the Covid-19 fundraiser special, how many episodes of Parks and Recreation have aired?

2. What year did Parks and Recreation first air?

3. What year was Amy Poehler born?

4. And what year was Nick Offerman born?

5. How many Golden Globes has Parks and Recreation won?

6. To the nearest hundred, how many minutes would the entirety of Parks and Recreation last for, if you were to play every single episode (again, including the special) back-to-back?

7. What is the financial value of the "Ron Swanson Scholarship" that allows Andy to attend a college course?

8. How many episodes has Amy Poehler either written or co-written?

9. In which number episode (overall, not just in the particular series) did Ben Wyatt and Chris Traeger first appear?

10. What date in 2015 did the Season 7 finale air?

11. What shirt number is on Andy's football jersey at his wedding to April?

12. How many times does Chris Traeger say the word "Literally" during the show?

13. How many times has Ron been married?

14. What age does Garry live to?

15. What percentage of the Lagavulin Distillery does Ron eventually own?

Answers on page 159

ANSWERS

Answer Sheet: Season 1

1. In the pilot episode, what injury has Andy sustained by falling into the pit? He's broken both of his legs.

2. What is the name of the town planner on whom Leslie has a crush? Mark Brendanawicz.

3. Shauna Mulwae-Tweep arrives at city council to interview members of the team about the pit construction project. What newspaper does she work for? The Pawnee Journal.

4. How many friends has the pit construction project earned on social media when the team first check it? Seven.

5. What gift to the department does Leslie initially confiscate as it is over $25 in value, but later enjoy, partially resulting in a letter being put on her file? A wine and cheese basket.

6. What possession of Andy's does Ann's neighbour steal from her house, prompting an injured, nude Andy to chase him through the street? Andy's boombox.

7. Tom tried to curry favour with Ron by deliberately losing to him at a particular online game. What is that game? Scramble.

8. What are the group of teenage boys throwing at each other when Leslie and Tom arrive to intervene? Plastic baggies of dog droppings.

9. What does Ron describe as "my number one favourite food, wrapped around my number three favourite food" while attending the awards banquet? Bacon-wrapped shrimp.

10. Who does Ron present an award to at the banquet? Leslie's mother.

11. What pick-up artist technique does Tom claim to be using, when he wears a goofy orange hat at the bar? Peacocking.

12. Tom's wife Wendy is introduced in the season finale. What is her job? She is a surgeon.

13. What does an annoyed Ann learn from a doctor at the hospital, in relation to Andy's recovery? He could have had his casts removed two weeks earlier, but, as Andy explains, he chose to keep them on because "I really, really like it when you serve me food".

14. How old is George Gernway, the man Leslie's mother sets her up on a date with? He is 62 years old (/young).

15. Who falls into the pit at the end of the season? Mark.

Answer Sheet: Leslie

1. What is Leslie's job title in the first few seasons of Parks and Recreation? Deputy Director of the Parks and Recreation Department.

2. Where does Ben propose to Leslie? In the house they were considering buying.

3. What is the subtitle to Leslie's book about Pawnee? 'The Greatest Town In America'.

4. Name three of the five women whose photographs Leslie displays on the wall next to her door. Hilary Clinton, Madeline Albright, Condoleezza Rice, Janet Reno and Nancy Pelosi.

5. How many shots of espresso does Leslie have in her coffee? Eight.

6. In which fictional town was Leslie Knope born? Eagleton, Indiana. (Pawnee hospital was overrun with raccoons at the time.)

7. What is Leslie Knope's mother's name? Marlene.

8. Who does the online dating service match Leslie with? Tom.

9. By what slender margin does Leslie bear Bobby Newport in the Season 4 city council election? 21 votes.

10. What type of animal does Leslie find "condescending"? Turtles.

11. What is Leslie's favourite restaurant? JJ's Diner.

12. When Andy is assigning code names to the group during the bus tour, what name does he give Leslie? "I'd Be Lying If I Said I Hadn't Thought About It".

13. Which former First Lady has Leslie met? Michelle Obama.

14. Who is number one on Leslie's 'sex list'? Joe Biden.

15. What are the names of Leslie and Ben's three children? Wesley, Stephen and Sonia.

Answer Sheet: Tom's Business Ideas

1. Snake Juice. The drink Tom created and sold in the Snake Lounge.

2. Saltweens. "Saltines for tweens".

3. Club-A-Dub-Dub or Clubmarine. A "sort of submarine-themed club".

4. Entertainment 720. A "premiere, high-end, all-media entertainment conglomerate so-named because "we go around the world twice for our clients".

5. Snail Mail. An "escargot delivery service".

6. Sparkle Suds. Detergent with glitter in it.

7. Disco Dairy. Butter with glitter.

8. Tommy Fresh. The fragrance he pitched to Dennis Feinstein.

9. Eclipse. A nightclub open for one hour, two times a year. Cover charge: $5000.

10. H2HO. A new brand of bottled water. That's it.

11. Rent-a-Swag. Pawnee's premier teen clothing rental service.

12. Yogurt Platinum. A gourmet alcoholic yogurt.

13. Tommy and the Foxx. A "raunchy animated series" based on Tom's non-existent friendship with Jamie Foxx.

14. Talking Tissues. A box of tissues that gives you a little message to hype you up every time a tissue is pulled out.

15. Know Ya Boo. A dating game show concept that sadly never got off the ground.

Answer Sheet: Ron

1. What is the name of Ron's jazz saxophonist alter ego? Duke Silver.

2. Who is Tammy Zero, in relation to Ron? She is his mother - the original Tammy.

3. What is Ron's middle name? Ulysses.

4. How old was Ron when he began work in a sheet metal factory? Nine years old. And "within two weeks, I was running the floor".

5. Tom reveals that when Ron has sex, he dresses like which sportsman the next day? Tiger Woods, wearing a red polo and black khaki pants.

6. What snack is known as a "Swanson" around Pawnee? A turkey leg wrapped in bacon.

7. How does Ron summarise his hamburger 'recipe'? "A hamburger made out of meat on a bun with nothing."

8. What is Ron's wife called? Diane.

9. Which family member does Ron reference when asked if his family had any history of mental illness? An uncle who "does yoga".

10. Ron claims to have cried only twice. When? Once when he was hit by a school bus at the age of 7, and once at Li'l Sebastian's memorial.

11. How many toes does Ron have? He has the toes he has. Let's just leave it at that. Let's just leave it at that.

12. What was the name of the building company run by Ron in Season 7? Very Good Building and Development Co.

13. What does Ron say is the only thing he hates more than lying? Skim milk, "which is water lying about being milk".

14. What is Ron's ringtone? A gunshot.

15. Which tennis star does Ron list as being one of his ideal women? Steffi Graf.

Answer Sheet: Season 2

1. How does Leslie cause controversy at Pawnee Zoo? She marries two male penguins.

2. What do Leslie and Tom discover has been planted in the new community garden? Marijuana.

3. Which two justifications does Councilman Bill Dexhart offer after he is found to have been engaging in four-way sex in a Brazilian cave while he was supposed to be building houses for the underprivileged? It was his birthday, and he really wanted to do it.

4. The Parks and Recreation department receives international visitors from a twin city of Pawnee. What country are the visitors from? Venezuela.

5. What is the name of the charity which arrives in Pawnee to build a playground in a single day? KaBOOM!

6. Why does Ron keep visiting Andy for shoe-shines? The polishing eases his bunion pain.

7. Which two members of the department are on the judging panel of the annual Miss Pawnee beauty pageant? Leslie and Tom.

8. What dinosaur-themed restaurant do the gang go to for a night out after Tom's divorce? Jurassic Fork.

9. Which member of the department discovers Ron's secret (jazz-related) double life, following a tip-off? Tom.

10. Which two characters appear in the cover photo of the Summer Events Catalog? Andy and April.

11. Which of the following do not visit Leslie's house during the party in which she is trying to impress Justin? A belly-dancer, a fencer, a judo master or an origami teacher? A judo master.

12. Who wins the Woman of the Year award? Ron.

13. On which date does April schedule 94 meetings for Ron, believing (incorrectly) that the date doesn't exist? March 31.

14. The penultimate episode of Season 2 sees two new characters join the show. Who are they? Ben Wyatt and Chris Traeger.

15. What is the name of the performer hired to sing at the annual children's concert? Freddy Spaghetti.

Answer Sheet: April

1. How old is April in Season 1? Nineteen.

2. What did April want to be as a child? A mortician.

3. What is April's sister called? Natalie.

4. What does April do for Andy to help make Ann jealous? She gives him some hickeys.

5. What is April's middle name, as revealed at her wedding to Andy? Roberta.

6. What was Andy's somewhat underwhelming reply when April said "I love you"? "Dude, shut up! That is Awesome-sauce!"

7. April created her own major in college. What was it? Halloween studies.

8. How long does April date Andy before they get married? One month.

9. What language does April speak (apart from English)? Spanish.

10. Where does April move to during Season 5? Washington D.C.

11. What is the name of the three-legged dog adopted by April and Andy? Champion.

12. What was the name of April's bisexual boyfriend? Derek.

13. What nickname did April's parents give her: TuTu, WuWu or ZuZu? ZuZu.

14. What song was playing when April gave birth? Monster Mash.

15. What is the name of April and Andy's son? Jack.

Answer Sheet: Who Said It?

1. "Just remember, every time you look up at the moon, I, too, will be looking at a moon. Not the same moon, obviously, That's impossible." Andy Dwyer.

2. "These dogs are so cute I want to throw up and kill myself." Craig Middlebrooks.

3. "Oh my god! [catches calculator] Hey, Dr. Buttons! …I mean, my old calculator. It doesn't have a name." Ben Wyatt.

4. "No matter what I do, literally nothing bad can happen to me. I'm like a white, male US Senator." Leslie Knope.

5. "If I keep my body moving, and my mind occupied at all times, I will avoid falling into a bottomless pit of despair." Chris Traeger.

6. "When Andy and I used to go the movies, he would always try to guess the ending of the movie. And he would always guess that the main character had been dead the whole time. Even when we saw Ratatouille." Ann Perkins.

7. "I once worked with a guy for three years and never learned his name. Best friend I ever had. We still never talk sometimes." Ron Swanson.

8. "Do I look like I drink water?" Donna Meagle.

9. "Most people would say 'the deets', but I say 'the tails'. Just another example of innovation." Tom Haverford.

10. "I didn't know I was adopted." Garry Gergich.

11. "Let the record show there was a standing ovation." Jeremy Jamm.

12. "Boss man, I wanna go home early. Ooh, hold on actually, hang on. Yeah, no, I wanna quit and never come here again." Mona Lisa Saperstein.

13. "I guess my thoughts on abortion are, you know, let's all just have a good time." Bobby Newport.

14. "Thank god my grandfather just died, so I am fluh-uh-shed with ca-ah-ash." Jean-Ralphio Saperstein.

15. "I wasn't listening but I strongly disagree with Ann." April Ludgate.

Answer Sheet: Andy

1. What is the main name of Andy's band? Mouse Rat.

2. What is the name of Andy's FBI alter ego? Bert Macklin. "Macklin, you son of a bitch."

3. Who was Andy's most regular customer at the shoeshine stand (though rarely received great customer service)? Kyle.

4. Which landmark do Andy and April visit in Season 3? The Grand Canyon.

5. What is the age gap between Andy and April? 8 years.

6. What does Andy diagnose Leslie with after trying to look up her symptoms on the internet? Network connectivity problems.

7. What did Andy claim was his favourite food? Butter.

8. Andy didn't actually sell his last car - what happened to it? He just forgot where he parked it.

9. Which part of the police entry examination does Andy fail: the physical test, the personality test or the written test? The personality test.

10. What is Andy's favourite football team? Indianapolis Colts.

11. What song did Andy write to celebrate the life of Li'l Sebastian? 5000 Candles in the Wind.

12. What did Andy study at college? Women's Studies.

13. What is the full name of Andy's children's entertainment television show? The Johnny Karate Super Awesome Musical Explosion Show.

14. Which British aristocrat does Andy befriend in Season 6? Lord Edgar Covington.

15. How does Andy explain his significant weight loss in Season 6? He quit drinking beer.

Answer Sheet: Season 3

1. Which two characters go head-to-head as coaches of Pawnee's only two junior league basketball teams? Ron and Andy.

2. What is the only item placed in the time capsule? A video recording of the public forum/argument to decide what would go in the capsule.

3. Which member of the Parks department does Ann bump into at the singles' mixer? Donna.

4. Where does Tom pitch his cologne to Dennis Feinstein? The Snakehole Lounge.

5. Leslie discovers a woman's razor and a pink swimming cap in Chris's bathroom, resulting in her telling Ann he is having an affair. What is Chris's explanation for the presence of the items? He shaves his legs with the razor for swimming, and the pink shower cap was for swimming in a breast cancer awareness triathlon.

6. Which radio duo catch Ben off-guard during an interview with questions about his time as a teenage mayor? Crazy Ira and the Douche.

7. Which Pawnee event does Leslie resurrect to help get the Parks department budget restored? The Harvest Festival.

8. Where does Ron reveal that he tends to buy most of his food? Food 'N Stuff. It's also where he buys most of his stuff.

9. Ron begins Season 3 dating Tom ex-wife Wendy, but they break up when she moves away. What country does she relocate to? Canada.

10. Who paints a depiction of Leslie as a powerful and bare-chested Greek goddess? Jerry.

11. What fitting birthday party does Leslie throw for Ron? Time alone with steak, whisky and his favourite movies.

12. Which band does April (briefly) tell Andy is her favourite (rather than his band)? Neutral Milk Hotel.

13. What does young girl Lauren write in response to her assignment "Why Government Matters", after spending the afternoon with Ron? "It doesn't".

14. What does Ron offer as a gift to Lauren to help her protect her property? A Claymore land mine.

15. Who gets singed by a fireball while attempting to light the eternal flame at Li'l Sebastian's memorial? Ron.

Answer Sheet: Tom

1. Which state is Tom from? South Carolina.

2. Which sport's reservation system does Tom have complete authority over, allowing him to meet female guests? The Pawnee tennis court reservation system.

3. Tom states that one of his pickup tactics is to give girls copies of his house keys and tell them to show up whenever. He says that no one has shown up so far, but how many times has he been robbed? Twice.

4. Where does Tom meet Lucy, who he is dating as of the Season 7 finale? She is a bartender at the Snake Hole Lounge.

5. Which of his colleagues does Tom accidentally shoot during the hunting trip? Ron.

6. What is the primary reason for Tom and Wendy getting divorced? It was a green card marriage and she has qualified for citizenship.

7. Which retail store is Tom working at, at the beginning of Season 3? Lady Foot Locker

8. Who does Tom sell the Rent-a-Swag business to? Dr. Saperstein.

9. Why does Leslie match with Tom on the online dating service? He runs multiple profiles to allow himself to match with pretty much every possible woman. Leslie matches with the "nerd" profile.

10. What is the name of the restaurant Tom opens? Tom's Bistro.

11. What name does Tom give his vacuum-cleaning, music-playing creation? DJ Roomba.

12. Where does Tom eventually take inspiration from when designing the new Parks department logo? Jerry's original employee ID card from the 1970s.

13. What does Tom claim is behind every successful man? "Me, smiling and taking partial credit."

14. How does Tom propose to Lucy? He writes "Will you marry me?" on a playing card which she picks from the deck during a card trick he is doing for her at the Snake Hole Lounge - a reference to their first date and where they met.

15. What was his original plan for the proposal? He shot a proposal action movie trailer with the 'help' of Jean-Ralphio.

Answer Sheet: The Ron Swanson Pyramid of Greatness

1. Canada. False.

2. Crying. True.

3. Torso. True.

4. Sickness Management. False.

5. Shelving. False.

6. Biceps. False.

7. Firearms. False.

8. Deer Protein. True.

9. Stillness. True.

10. Romantic Love. True.

11. Testicles. False.

12. Ability to Create Fire. False.

13. Gold. False.

14. Old Wooden Sailing Ships. True.

15. Poise. True.

Answer Sheet: Chris

1. What is the name of Chris's therapist? Dr. Richard Nygard.

2. What does Chris say is his resting heart rate: 13, 23 or 33 beats per minute? 23. "The scientists who study me say my heart could pump jet fuel up into an airplane."

3. What event from his past does Chris put his relentless positivity down to? He was diagnosed with a rare blood disorder as a baby and was not expected to live longer than three weeks, but miraculously survived - so he sees every day as a gift.

4. Who does Chris go to Andy and April's Halloween party dressed as? Sherlock Holmes.

5. What is the name of Jerry's daughter, whom Chris dates for a while? Millicent.

6. What is Chris's job when he first enters the show? He is a State Auditor for Indiana.

7. And what job does he take, that sees him stay in Pawnee more permanently? City Manager.

8. What is Chris's body fat percentage? (We'll accept the nearest whole number if you want to guess.) 2.8%.

9. What type of burger does Chris make in an (unsuccessful) attempt to beat Ron's hamburger? A lean turkey burger.

10. What is unusual about the new desk Chris gives to Ron? It is circular, forcing him to interact with people approaching him from all angles.

11. When Andy assigns each member of the department a code name during the bus tour, what does he label Chris? "If I Had To Pick A Dude".

12. When Ann confronts Chris about her suspicions he is cheating on her, he is surprised. Why? He had broken up with her some time earlier, but was so cheery and enthusiastic while doing it that she didn't realise.

13. What 'candy' does Chris offer the group when they are waiting hungrily for Ron's barbecue? Raisins. AKA nature's candy.

14. When Chris is preparing to move back to Indianapolis, who does he ask to come with him? April. (As his assistant.)

15. What song does Chris use to showcase his (limited) vocal abilities when acting as a backing vocalist on Andy's campaign song? "Take Me Out to the Ball Game".

Answer Sheet: Season

1. What is the name of the youth camp run by Leslie? Pawnee Goddesses.

2. Who emails a photograph of their genitals to all of the female employees at City Hall? Sewage Joe from the sewage department.

3. How long does Ron go to hide in the wilderness for, after learning Tammy One has arrived in town? 180 days.

4. How does Leslie escape more severe punishment for her secret relationship with Ben? Ben takes full responsibility and resigns from his role as Assistant City Manager.

5. Which territory does April play as in the Model United Nations conference? The moon.

6. What gift is Ben trying to give Leslie when she flees into the woods to hide with Ron? A "Knope 2012" button, to celebrate her running for office.

7. What is the name of Leslie's campaign song, written by Andy? Catch Your Dream. Some great sax work by Ron on the recording, too.

. How long is the claymation film produced by Ben when he premieres it to Chris? 10 seconds. It's mostly credits, with only two seconds of actual claymation.

9. What is the name of Bobby Newport's campaign manager? Jennifer Barkley.

10. What alcohol do Tammy Zero and Tammy One use for their "prairie drink-off"? A very strong Swanson family mash liquor.

11. April drives Andy to see the Grand Canyon to check off one of his bucket-list items, but what landmark was he actually thinking of? Mount Rushmore.

12. Who does Ann go on a date with on Valentine's Day? Tom.

13. Who was the pie that hits Jerry in the face actually intended for? Ben. It was thrown by Sewage Joe in retribution for his sacking.

14. Whose birthday gets forgotten (and belatedly celebrated) during Leslie's campaign? Jerry's. Of course.

15. Who accidentally deletes all of the department's files? April. Luckily Donna saves the day with the back-up system she put in place to Jerry-proof their infrastructure.

Answer Sheet: Ben

1. What town was Ben elected mayor of while still a teenager? Partridge, Minnesota.

2. How did he accidentally bankrupt the city? He invested all of their funds into creating a winter sports complex called Ice Town.

3. What is Ben's favourite food? Calzones.

4. What nickname does Jean-Ralphio give Ben? Jello-shot.

5. When Andy assigns each member of the department a code name during the bus tour, what is Ben given? "Eagle Two".

6. What does Ben buy to cheer himself up while on a "Treat Yo' Self" outing with Donna and Tom? A full Batman costume.

7. What is the name of the claymation film Ben works on during downtime after his resignation? "Requiem for a Tuesday".

8. What fantasy memorabilia item does Leslie gift to Ben for their anniversary? The Iron Throne from Game of Thrones.

9. Who does Ben take on as his assistant when he starts working for Sweetums? Andy.

10. With which Cones of Dunshire piece does Ben ultimately beat Gryzzl's founder in their duel to get Pawnee accepted into Gryzzl's WiFi initiative? His farmer. His humble farmer.

11. Which board game is Ben a "nationally ranked" player of? Settlers of Catan.

12. What authoritarian figures does Ben have a huge fear of? Police officers.

13. Who does Ben spend his and Leslie's first anniversary with, enjoying a couple's massage, a horse-drawn carriage ride and tango lessons? Jerry.

14. What does the accounting firm give Ben as a leaving present? The copyright to the Cones of Dunshire board game.

15. What British honour is bestowed on Ben by Lord Covington in The Johnny Karate Super Awesome Musical Explosion Show? Member of the Order of the British Empire (MBE).

Answer Sheet: Andy's Band Names

1. Crackfinger. True.

2. Frightshaft. False.

3. Threeskin. True.

4. Ninjadick. True.

5. Ham Dragon. False.

6. Psych Ass. False.

7. Jet Black Pope. True.

8. God Hates Figs. True.

9. Department of Homeland Obscurity. True.

10. The Kind Man's Cruellest Secret. False.

11. Muscle Confusion. True.

12. The Museum of Natural Fistery. False.

13. Flames for Flames. True.

14. Man Feelings. False.

15. The Clone Harbourers. False.

Answer Sheet: Donna

1. What is Donna's job in the Parks department? Office Manager.

2. What is the name of Donna's famous musician cousin? Ginuine.

3. What type of car does Donna own? A Mercedes-Benz.

4. Which band wrote an album about Donna, as revealed at her wedding to Joe? Pearl Jam. It was Vitalogy, apparently.

5. What type of business does Donna found on leaving the Parks department? (Bonus point if you can remember the name of the business.) Real estate, with her company Regal Meagle Realty.

6. What does Donna work as between the government shutdown and its reopening in the opening episode of Season 3? She sells rubber nipples via telephone.

7. Donna's grandma was a fan of the menfolk, and her dating advice to Donna was "use him, abuse him, lose him". But how did she die? Grammy Meagle died at the age of 84, sandwiched between two 30 year-olds.

8. What is Donna's husband's job? He is a teacher.

9. What is Donna's simple rule when it comes to dating football players? "Skill positions only."

10. Legally, what is the maximum number of members of Donna's family that can be on an international flight together at the same time? Three.

11. What is Donna's favourite TV show, which she bonds with Craig over? Scandal.

12. Which feature of which character, combined with Donna's "everything else", would make their hypothetical child unstoppable? Chris's hair.

13. What is the name of Donna's (and Ron's) hairdresser, who later marries Craig Middlebrooks? Typhoon.

14. What is the name of Donna's brother, whom she hates? Lavondrius.

15. Which Oscar-winning actress auditioned for the role of Donna? Octavia Spencer.

Answer Sheet: Season 5

1. Whose words of comfort does Leslie rebuff while sulking in the coatroom at a cocktail party? John McCain.

2. What is the name of the pig which Ron brings to the barbecue? Tom.

3. How does Ron meet Diane? She calls Chris's new hotline to request that someone fix a pothole in front of her house. Ron is the man for the job.

4. What does April want to turn Lot 48 into? A dog park.

5. What is the first (sugar-related) bill Leslie tries to pass in city council? The soda tax.

6. How do Leslie and April manage to dispose of the huge refrigerator the garbage team were unable to lift? They arrange for a local soup kitchen to pick it up.

7. What does April give Leslie as a present after their time spent working as garbage collectors? A gift box filled with trash.

8. Ron, Chris and Ben all catch food-poisoning when choosing a caterer for the wedding. Why is Tom, who was also in attendance, unaffected? He didn't eat the calzones.

9. Which potential candidate announces Ann's sperm donor hunt on the radio? The Douche.

10. Where do Leslie and Ben get married? City Hall.

11. Who crashes the wedding, before being gently suppressed by Ron? Councilman Jamm.

12. What is the name of the business that pops up to rival Rent-a-Swag? Tommy's Closet.

13. What does Chris tell Ann is his spirit animal: a jaguar, a lion, a woodmouse or a hare? A jaguar.

14. Who does Ann ultimately decide to have a baby with? Chris.

15. What type of business does Leslie bail out, resulting in it taking a somewhat seedier direction? A movie rental store called the Video Dome.

Answer Sheet: Garry

1. What is Garry's actual first name? (Clue: it isn't Garry.) Gerald.

2. What is Garry's wife named? Gayle.

3. How many daughters does Garry have? Three.

4. In Season 2, an injured Garry claims to have been mugged in the park. What really happened? He dropped a breakfast burrito in a creek, then fell while trying to grab it and dislocated his shoulder.

5. What year was Garry born: 1948, 1950 or 1952? 1948

6. Ron describes Garry (then Jerry) as both the "schlemiel" and the "schlemazel" of the office. What does this mean? That Garry is both the person who spills the soup and is the person upon whom the soup is spilled.

7. What misdemeanour does policeman Dave reveal Jerry has committed on a number of occasions? Public urination violations.

8. What is Garry's favourite holiday destination? Muncie, Indiana.

9. When Garry suffered a heart attack and extreme flatulence simultaneously after being surprised by Leslie and Ann, what was Tom's diagnosis? That Garry had a fart attack.

10. Why did Donna, Tom, Andy and April not receive their invitations to Garry's family party? They had "Jerry filters" set up on their computer to avoid having to read his emails.

11. What musical instrument does Garry play? Piano.

12. What does Garry accidentally get printed as the background image on Tom's restaurant menus? Pictures of his dog's rectum, intended for the vet.

13. What date is Garry's birthday? February 29th, hence the 'Sweet Sixteen' party for his 64th birthday.

14. How many terms does Garry go on to serve as mayor of Pawnee? 10.

15. True or false: Garry's surname is spelt incorrectly on his headstone? True. It's spelt as 'Girgich' rather than 'Gergich'.

Answer Sheet: Anagrams

1. Overdraft Ohm? Tom Haverford.

2. Be Brown By Pot? Bobby Newport.

3. Managed Lone? Donna Meagle.

4. Graduate Pill? April Ludgate.

5. Spanner Ink? Ann Perkins.

6. New Batty? Ben Wyatt.

7. Yawned Dry? Andy Dwyer.

8. China Mop? Champion.

9. Elope Likens? Leslie Knope.

10. Right Careers? Chris Traeger.

11. Liable Stains? Li'l Sebastian.

12. Hardly Peep? Perd Hapley.

13. Sworn Anons? Ron Swanson. Kind of fitting.

14. Canola Jazz Mole? Joan Calamezzo.

15. Gig Rag Cherry? Garry Gergich.

Answer Sheet: Tom's Nicknames for Things

1. "Zerts". Desserts.

2. "Tray-trays". Entrees.

3. "Sammies". Sandwiches.

4. "Big ol' cookies". Cakes.

5. "Cool blasterz". Air conditioners. He doesn't know where the Z came from.

6. "Sandoozles". Sandwiches.

7. "Long ass rice". All noodles.

8. "Fri-fri chicky-chick". Fried chicken.

9. "Chicky catch". Chicken cacciatore.

10. "Adam Sandlers". Sandwiches. He has a lot of different names for sandwiches.

11. "Pre-birds". Eggs. He also calls them future birds.

12. "Super water". Root beer.

13. "Bean blankies". Tortillas.

14. "Food rakes". Forks.

15. "Go-go mobile". Car.

Answer Sheet: Season 6

1. What city do Leslie, Ben, Ron, April and Andy visit for the first two episodes? London.

2. Who is maid of honour at Ron and Diane's wedding? Leslie.

3. Where do Ann and Chris move to from Pawnee? Michigan.

4. Who accidentally uses the Parks department's Twitter handle for a sex-themed tweet? Donna.

5. Why does Tom decide to get his wine cellar soundproofed? He hires shouty Craig as his sommelier.

6. What is released when Leslie tears down the wall separating Pawnee and Eagleton? A swarm of bees.

7. What does Ann call her baby? Oliver.

8. What is the name of Annabel Porter's internet lifestyle magazine that labels Ron's handmade chairs as a trend? Bloosh.

9. What does April finally decide is Donna's spirit dog? A cat.

10. What do Ron and Diane name their son? John Swanson.

11. Who comes up with Andy's stage name when he's providing children's entertainment? Craig Middlebrooks.

12. What do the guys gift to Chris as a leaving present? A buddy-box, crafted by Ron and emblazoned with their initials, to fill with memories for his child.

13. Which local celebrity do Leslie and Ann get to endorse the new Sweetums sports drink, as part of the chain of events that will allow them to gain access to Lot 48? Perd Hapley.

14. Which musical event takes place at the finale of the season? The Pawnee/Eagleton Unity Concert.

15. And which establishment holds its grand opening shortly after that event? Tom's Bistro.

Answer Sheet: Leslie's Romantic Descriptions of Ann

1. "Ann, you beautiful tropical fish." True.

2. "Ann, you beautiful, naive, sophisticated newborn baby." True.

3. "Ann, you wistful, fragrant tiger lily." False.

4. "Ann, you cunning, pliable, chestnut-haired sunfish." True.

5. "Ann, you rainbow-infused space unicorn." True.

6. "Ann, you freshly-bathed crab-hustler." False.

7. "Ann, you beautiful spinster." True.

8. "Ann, you opalescent tree-shark." True.

9. "Ann, you benevolent, whispering clam." False.

10. "Ann, you poetic, noble land-mermaid." True.

11. "Ann, you heroic, gloriously-tousled capybara." False.

12. "Ann, you rare, glorious deer-queen." False.

13. "Ann, you glossy, Parisian sea-otter." False.

14. "Ann, you beautiful, rule-breaking moth." True.

15. "Ann, you beautiful, talented, brilliant, powerful musk-ox." True.

Answer Sheet: Complete the Quote

1. "Strippers do nothing for me…but I will take a _____ _____ _____ anytime, anyplace." - Ron. "Free breakfast buffet".

2. "We have to remember what's important in life: friends, _____ and work. Or _____, friends and work. But work has to come third." - Leslie. "Waffles".

3. "Sometimes you gotta work a little so you can _____ a lot." - Tom. "Ball".

4. "I think that _____ _____ always screams 'fun', right?" - Jerry/Garry. "Comic sans".

5. "I don't know who _____ _____ is, and at this point I'm too afraid to ask." - Andy. "Al Gore".

6. "It's like I always say. When life gives you lemons, you sell some of your _____'s _____, and go clubbing." - Jean-Ralphio. "Grandma's jewellery".

7. "Crying: Acceptable at funerals and the _____ _____." - Ron. "Grand Canyon".

8. "I made my money the old-fashioned way. I got run over by a _____!" - Jean-Ralphio. "Lexus".

9. "On a scale from one to _____ _____, how p*ssed off is he?" - Tom. "Chris Brown".

10. "No offence, but I don't remember you having a nursing degree in _____." - Leslie. "Feelings".

11. "It's like dealing with a strict mother. Who I am confusingly attracted to. Ben is like _____ _____." - Leslie. "A MILF".

12. "I don't get anything until I'm 50, which is a waste because I'm going to be a billionaire in Costa Rica by then. Eatin' dolphin and hangin' out with _____ _____." - Jean-Ralphio. "Lady singers".

13. "April is the best. But she's 20. When April was born, I was already in the third grade, which means if we were friends back then, I would have been hanging out with a baby. I don't know anything about _____ _____." - Andy. "Infant care".

14. "As Leslie's Maid of Honor, I really need her bachelorette party to go well, which is why I'm stress-eating these _____ _____." - Ann. "Gummy penises".

15. "I love Chinese crap. Lucy Liu, Gangnam Style, Nintendo, _____, etc, etc." - Jeremy Jamm. "Sushi".

Answer Sheet: Season 7

1. What was the Morning Star referenced in the "Morning Star Incident"? The building erected by Ron on the site of Lot 48 and where Ann's old home used to be, resulting in a rift between he and Leslie.

2. What is the value of the bid Leslie places to buy land from the wealthy Newport family to create a national park? $0.

3. Who is seduced by Tammy Two? Jamm.

4. Who gets inducted into the Pawnee "Walk of Fame"? Joan Callamezzo.

5. What is the name of the tech company that begins to take over Pawnee? Gryzzl.

6. What is the name of Tammy Two's perfume? "Girth".

7. Who is Donna's maid of honour? April.

8. Which two characters pass away in the episode 'Two Funerals'? Mayor Walter Gunderson and Ron's barber, Salvatore.

9. Who becomes the new landlord of JJ's Diner? Dennis Feinstein.

10. Who manages to negotiate ownership of the rights to Johnny Karate for Andy? Tom. After a lot of crying.

11. Which of these items did not appear on Craig's list of Great Things About Being Alive: watermelon martinis, exposed brick, Jennifer Love Hewitt or air-dried beech beams? Air-dried beech beams.

12. In the finale, who is shown to go on to become a best-selling author? Tom.

13. Which two characters fake their own death? Jean-Ralphio and Mona Lisa.

14. What is the name of the online learning initiative Donna sets up with her husband? "Teach Yo' Self".

15. What is the final line spoken in the season, by Leslie? "I'm ready."

Answer Sheet: Cast & Crew

1. Which two people created the show? Greg Daniels and Michael Schur.

2. Who was the first main cast member to direct an episode? Amy Poehler.

3. Which Mad Men star cameos as an incompetent member of the National Parks Service? Jon Hamm.

4. Who plays Chris Traeger? Rob Lowe.

5. Who plays Ann Perkins? Rashida Jones.

6. Who plays Tom Haverford? Aziz Ansari.

7. Who plays Bobby Newport? Paul Rudd.

8. Which two Brooklyn Nine-Nine stars cameo? Chelsea Peretti and Andy Samberg.

9. Who plays Ben Wyatt? Adam Scott.

10. Which Good Place star appears in Parks and Recreation as an Eagleton councilwoman? Kristen Bell.

11. What was considered as a title for the sitcom, before being rejected by network executives who didn't want to make fun of local government? Public Service.

12. Which Arrested Development star appears as an MRI consultant who goes on a date with Leslie? Will Arnett.

13. Who cameos during one of Tom and Donna's Treat Yo' Self days, ordering the sushi named after himself at a Beverly Hills restaurant? Josh Groban.

14. Who plays Donna Meagle? Retta.

15. Which network did Seasons 1-7 originally air on? NBC.

Answer Sheet: Special

1. What date in 2020 did the episode air? April 30.

2. Who is the first character to appear in the special? Bobby Newport.

3. What platform are the group using to carry out their video calls? Gryzzl.

4. Who keeps getting skipped over in the call tree? Garry.

5. What service does Jeremy Jamm advertise? Home dental delivery.

6. While under the influence of cleaning supplies, Ben plans to combine two of his greatest creations during lockdown. What does he plan to make? A claymation film based on his board game The Cones of Dunshire.

7. How frequently is Chris donating blood? Four times a week.

8. And what does Chris say is his blood type? "Just… positive".

9. Where is Andy trapped? His own shed.

10. Who keeps accidentally applying filters to their video calls?
Garry.

11. Where in the world does Tom claim to be, with the assistance of
a virtual background? Bali.

12. What illustrious collective of awards does Joan Calamezzo claim
to have obtained? EGOT. "You've got an EGOT?" "Yes, I've been
banned from all four ceremonies."

13. During the video calls, what is on the shelves behind Donna
(when she doesn't join Tom in the virtual background destination)?
Many, many sneakers. Perhaps an outcome of a Treat Yo' Self day?

14. Which intruder did Ron catch in his cabin? Tammy Two. What a
joy that husband-and-wife Nick Offerman and Megan Mullally live
together, allowing that reveal to happen.

15. Which song do the characters sing for Leslie at the end of the
episode? 500 Candles in the Wind. Of course.

Answer Sheet: Tiebreakers

1. Including the Covid-19 fundraiser special, how many episodes of Parks and Recreation have aired? 126.

2. What year did Parks and Recreation first air? 2009.

3. What year was Amy Poehler born? 1971.

4. And what year was Nick Offerman born? 1970.

5. How many Golden Globes has Parks and Recreation won? 1 - by Amy Poehler for Best Actress in a Television Series Musical or Comedy.

6. To the nearest hundred, how many minutes would the entirety of Parks and Recreation last for, if you were to play every single episode (again, including the special) back-to-back? 2700 minutes. We're game if you are.

7. What is the financial value of the "Ron Swanson Scholarship" that allows Andy to attend a college course? $940.

8. How many episodes has Amy Poehler either written or co-written? Five.

9. In which number episode (overall, not just in the particular series) did Ben Wyatt and Chris Traeger first appear? 29.

10. What date in 2015 did the Season 7 finale air? February 15.

11. What shirt number is on Andy's football jersey at his wedding to April? 87.

12. How many times does Chris Traeger say the word "Literally" during the show? 41.

13. How many times has Ron been married? Four. Once to Tammy One, twice to Tammy Two and once to Diane.

14. What age does Garry live to? 100, and he dies surrounded by his adoring family.

15. What percentage of the Lagavulin Distillery does Ron eventually own? 51%.

Printed in Great Britain
by Amazon

49048311R10078